THE LITTLE ELEPHANT

by YLLA

STORY BY Arthur Gregor

Designed by Luc Bouchage

A HARPER TROPHY PICTURE BOOK

HARPER & ROW, PUBLISHERS New York, Hagerstown, San Francisco, London

THE LITTLE ELEPHANT
Copyright © 1956 by Harper & Row, Publishers, Inc.
Printed in the U.S.A. All rights reserved.
Library of Congress Catalog Card Number: 56-8140

Japu, the little elephant, had a dream.

"What a beautiful dream," he thought, as he woke up.

That morning, the children from the town came and told him that everybody was getting ready for the King's parade. They told him of the flags on the rooftops and the flowers in the windows of all the houses. When Japu heard this, he remembered his dream.

He had dreamed he had gone to the King's parade. He had dreamed he had stood in front of the King's palace, which was all lit up and looked like a house blazing with stars. He had dreamed that the King had smiled at him, and that it was he, little Japu, who led the parade, as the musicians played.

And now the children begged him: "You must come to the parade. Will you come?"

There was no one in the forest the children loved as much as Japu.

Sadly, Japu nodded, yes, he would come. He wanted very much to go, but he knew what the children didn't know. He was still so little he couldn't walk very far. But he didn't want to disappoint the children, and he remembered how, in his dream, the musicians had played.

"Can I go to the parade?" he asked his mother shyly.

"To go to the parade," she said, "you must first become strong and great like your father."

His father, everyone said, walked like a king in the King's parade.

"First," said his mother, "you must learn to bathe in the river."

But the river was far, and Japu was still little.

He could walk only a short distance, and no more.

But his mother wrapped her trunk around him...

...and with her help they went on their way.

When they got to the river
his father was already there
with his friends,
and with his friends
were their little elephants.

At first, Japu didn't like the water. He had never washed in a river before. But now he saw that the other little elephants were having fun. They filled their trunks with water and sprayed it over themselves and over the grownups.

The grownups had gone into the water to wash themselves so they would be clean for the parade.

"Ah!" thought Japu. "The parade."

And again he remembered his dream, and this time he remembered how, in his dream, the King had smiled at him.

"Oh," he thought, "if only I could go."

And he wished to go so much, he forgot he didn't like the water.

He began to enjoy the water and joined the other little elephants.

Without their help, he jumped with them over the big elephants.

He ran out, dried himself in the grass and played with the others.

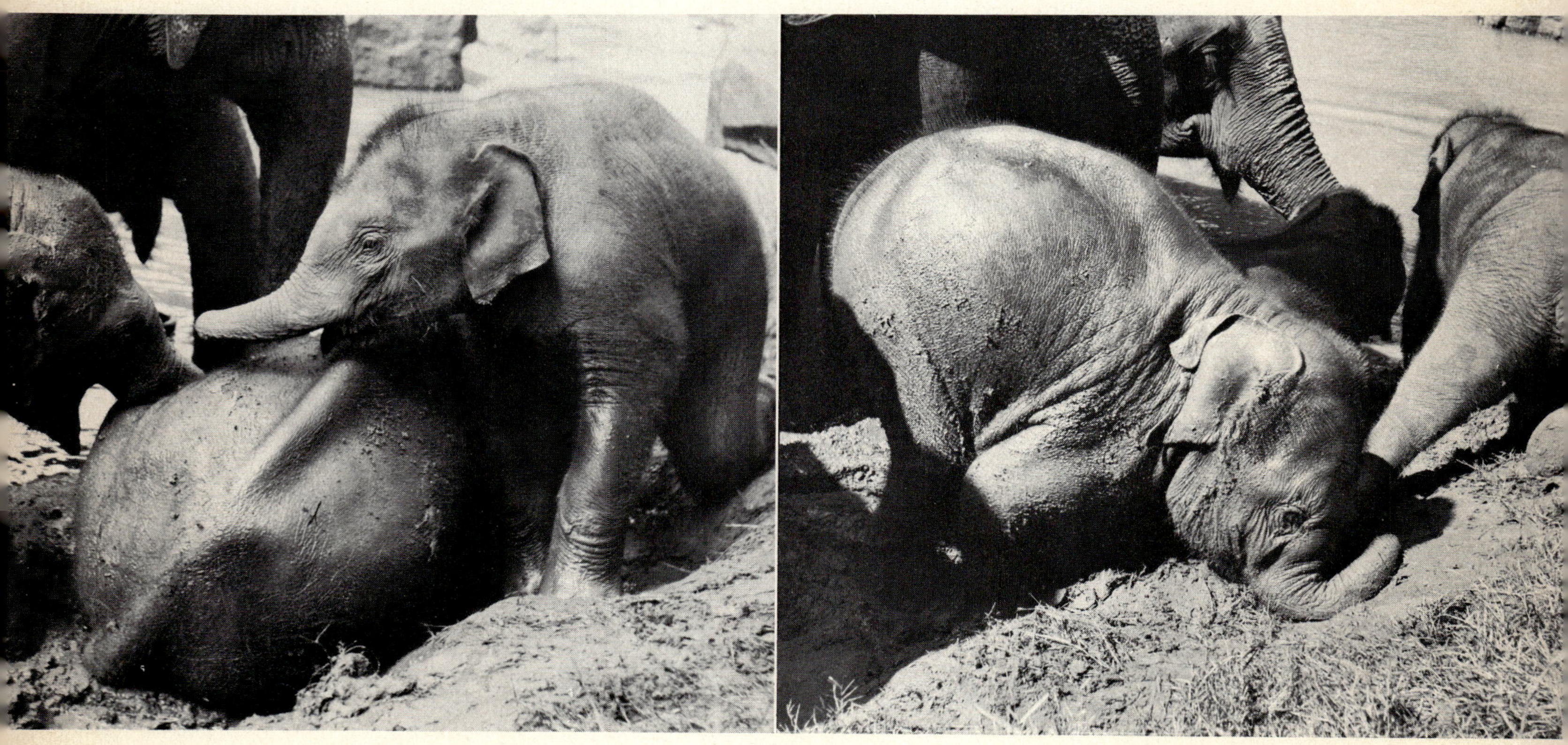

Hearing his dream like music in his head, he was very brave.

He played the game of fighting, was pushed down but got up again, and played

until they were exhausted.   The others lay on the ground, but Japu walked away.

He walked back to his mother and father. Brave little Japu could hardly believe he had done all these things by himself, and his mother and father could hardly believe he had done these things all by himself.

"How quickly he has learned to bathe in the river and to have fun with the others," said his mother.

And they agreed they wanted to do something to show Japu how pleased they were with him.

"I have a wonderful idea," his father said. "Why not take him to the parade?"

"He would certainly like that, but do you think he can now walk well enough to keep up with a parade?"

"We'll see about that," his father said. "If he can walk a stretch all by himself, then we can take him to the parade. Walk ahead, little elephant, walk ahead."

And all by himself Japu walked. Remembering again his dream, and this time how brightly lit the palace had seemed to him, he walked a long way, a very long way along the water.

"Good, Japu, very good." Japu had made his father proud of him.

"Good, my Japu, very good. Now you may come with us," his mother said, and she was very pleased to please him.

The whole town was getting ready for the parade, and when the children saw Japu, they were very glad.

"Japu has come," they cheered, "Japu has come."

And Japu nodded, yes, I have come. And the children had prepared for him rice mixed with milk, the dish Japu liked best of all.

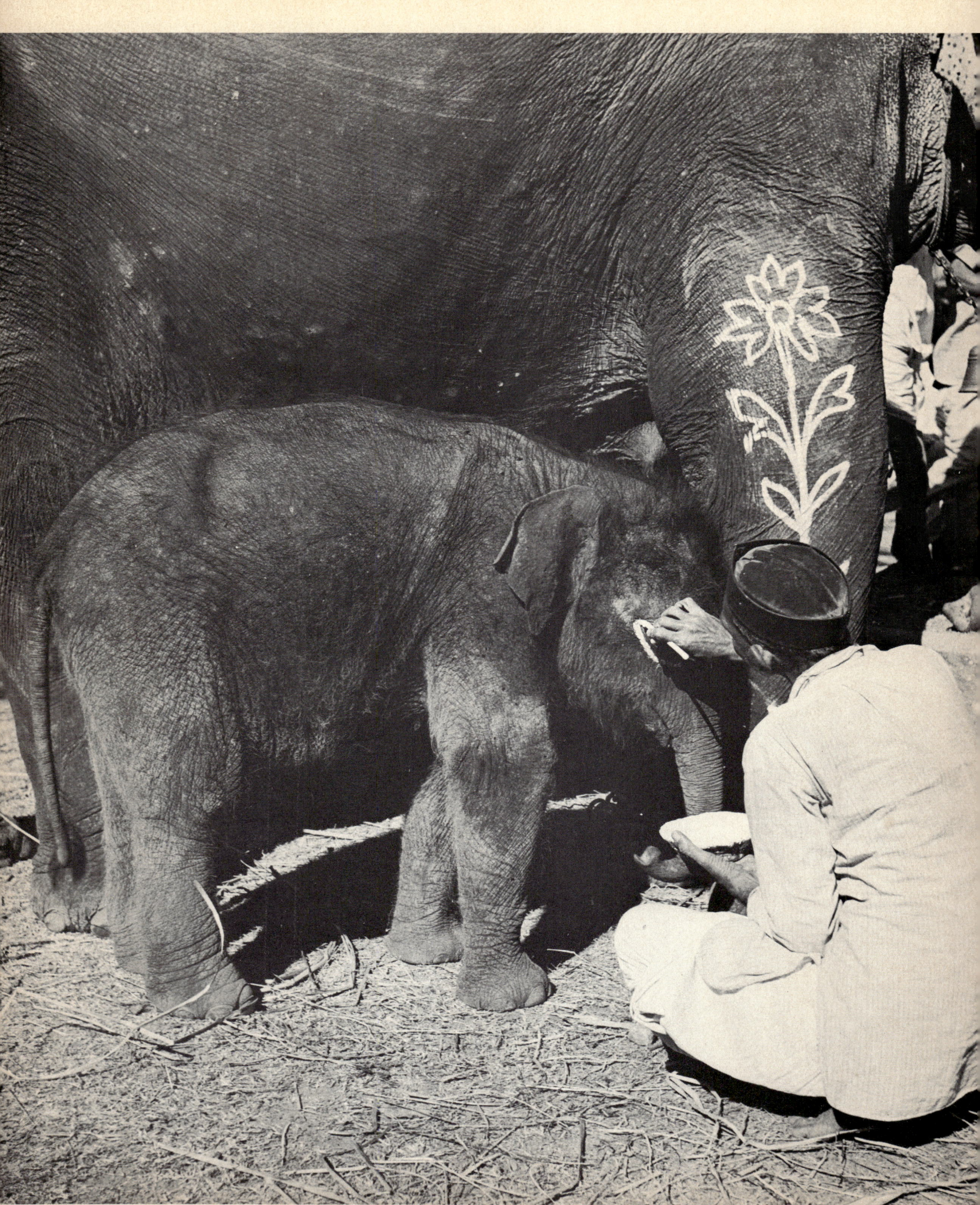

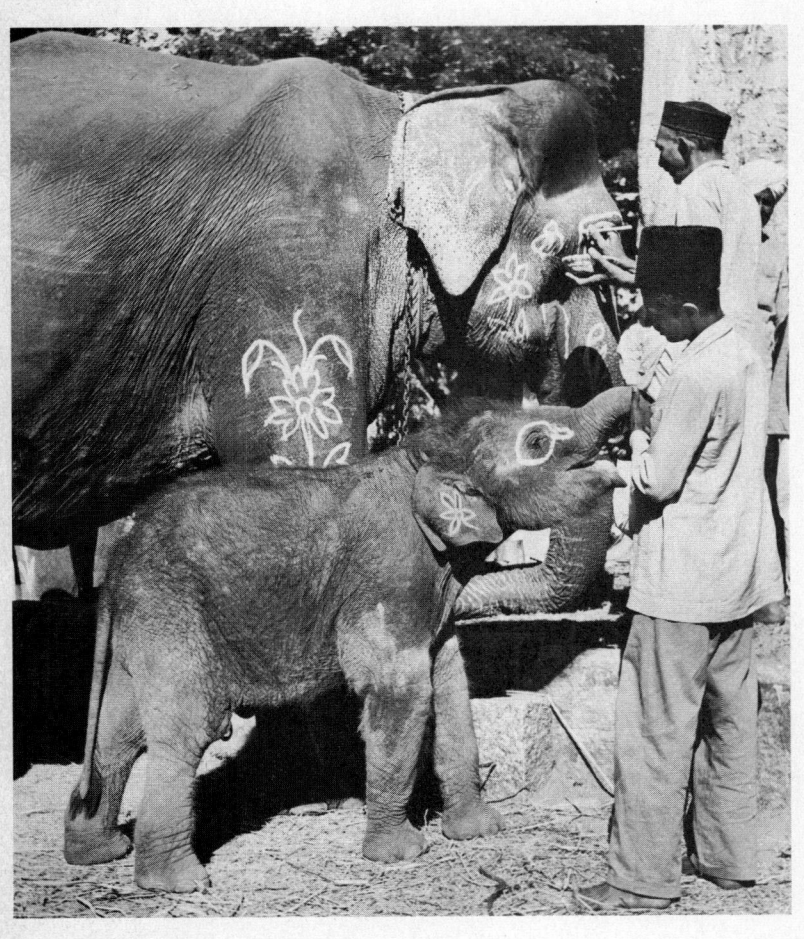

And then men came to decorate the three of them. They painted flowers on their legs and on their heads, flowers with leaves and long stems, and dressed Japu's mother and father for the parade.

Japu was very happy to see his mother dressed so wonderfully. And when he looked at his father, he thought:

"Now I know what they mean when they say my father is great."

And Japu said: "Now you look like a king in the King's parade."

And little Japu was so proud, so very proud of them both.

And so dazzled was he by everything that had happened, by everything that surrounded him, by the King's palace, the King's guards and the King's musicians, that he said: "It is more beautiful than my dream."

And how happy were the children to see him. And when the King came out on his balcony, and everyone began to sing a greeting to the King, the King smiled at Japu and sent a messenger to him to say that the King was very glad Japu had come. Everyone looked at Japu. The message also said:

Would Japu be the one to lead the parade? And so Japu became the first little elephant to walk ahead of all the other elephants in the King's parade, while all the King's musicians played. And everyone who saw him said: "One day Japu will be as good as his mother, and as great as his father."

Walk ahead, little elephant, walk ahead.

Books by YLLA available in Harper Trophy Picture Books

JP13 **ANIMAL BABIES**
Photographs by Ylla. Story by Arthur Gregor
Playful tiger cubs, a tiny waddling hippopotamus, cuddling baby monkeys, a procession of ducklings and many more young animals are lovingly watched over by their larger mothers. "An appealing and informative substitute for trips to farm or zoo."
—ALA *The Booklist*

JP14 **THE LITTLE ELEPHANT**
Photographs by Ylla. Story by Arthur Gregor
The little elephant's dream comes true when he leads the King's glorious parade. "Ylla's photographs are unmatched in sharpness of texture and the natural charm of animals caught in action."—*The Horn Book*

JP15 **THE SLEEPY LITTLE LION**
Photographs by Ylla. Story by Margaret Wise Brown
A small and very sleepy lion cub investigates as much of the world as he can stay awake to see. "A very simple text is interpreted by exceptionally appealing photographs."
—*Basic Books for Elementary School Libraries*

JP16 **TWO LITTLE BEARS**
Photographs and story by Ylla.
The two bears forget their mother's warning, and wander farther and farther until they are lost. "Everyone loves a baby, human or bear, and this book about two bear cubs is one that any child will love and want for his own."—*Saturday Review*